Making + MATH + *Work*

What Are the Chances?

BY JOY VISTO

CREATIVE EDUCATION

CREATIVE PAPERBACKS

Published by Creative Education and Creative Paperbacks
P.O. Box 227, Mankato, Minnesota 56002
Creative Education and Creative Paperbacks
are imprints of The Creative Company
www.thecreativecompany.us

Design and production by Liddy Walseth
Art direction by Rita Marshall
Printed in the United States of America

Photographs by Corbis (Roger Wood), Dreamstime (Rangizzz, Shevs), Getty Images
(Creative Crop, Dorling Kindersley), iStockphoto (bpalmer, Cimmerian, DebbiSmirnoff,
iLexx, imagoRB, Diane Labombarbe, Maica, Mitroshkin, OSTILL, robtek, Rouzes, rusm,
Linda Steward, timmy, walrusmail), Shutterstock (Arkady Mazor, ostill, seamuss)
Vector illustrations by Donny Gettinger

Library of Congress Cataloging-in-Publication Data
Visto, Joy.
What are the chances? / Joy Visto.
p. cm. — (Making math work)
Includes bibliographical references and index.
Summary: A helpful guide for understanding the mathematical concepts and real-world
applications of probability and statistics, including classroom tips, common terms such
as outliers, and exercises to encourage hands-on practice.
ISBN 978-1-60818-573-3 (hardcover)
ISBN 978-1-62832-174-6 (pbk)
1. Probabilities—Juvenile literature. 2. Mathematical statistics—Juvenile literature. I. Title.

QA273.16.V57 2015
519.2—dc23 2014034726

CCSS: RI.5.1, 2, 3, 8; RI.6.1, 2, 3, 4, 5, 6, 7; RST.6-8.3, 4, 6, 7

First Edition HC 9 8 7 6 5 4 3 2 1
First Edition PBK 9 8 7 6 5 4 3 2 1

When you think about mathematics, you probably think about a class at school where you do **calculations** and answer word problems. But have you ever thought about math being all around you? It's in every shape and pattern you see. It's in every song you hear. It's in every game you play and any puzzle you solve! The first mathematicians realized this, and they looked for ways to prove it—to show how order and reason could explain much about life as they knew it. Sometimes this was easy to do. But other times, people just didn't get it. Even some of the most intelligent people in history have struggled with math: Albert Einstein once wrote to a child, "Do not worry about your difficulties in Mathematics. I can assure you mine are still greater."

So how can you use whatever you know about math in everyday life? When you *wonder* about the *odds* of having a snow day, calculate your *average* test score, determine the *range* of options for an ice cream sundae, or flip a coin to make a decision, you are using math! These actions are part of a branch of mathematics known as probability and statistics. This is one of the newest branches of mathematics. It involves predicting how likely it is that particular events will occur and then studying them once they have happened. Think about the different events in your life. *What are* the ways you can apply probability and statistics to them?

Prominent American Series

ALBERT EINSTEIN
MATHEMATICIAN–PHYSICIST
NOBEL PRIZE WINNER
1879–1955

8c

Artmaster

First Day of Issue

FINDING MATH IN RANDOMNESS

IF YOU ARE FORCED TO DECIDE BETWEEN TWO SITUATIONS but aren't sure which to choose, you might do any number of things to narrow your options. You might flip a coin, you might roll a die, or you might even play a game of eeny, meeny, miney, moe. People have used similar games of chance for thousands of years.

Members of ancient civilizations such as the Greeks, Romans, and Babylonians played such games. However, they were not involved in learning the math behind those games. Probability, the study of how likely a given event is to occur, did not come about until the 1500s. The math used for determining probability is not very challenging, so it may seem odd that mathematicians did not figure it out for so long. They were definitely capable of doing the necessary calculations. Many mathematicians of the ancient world were studying **trigonometry** or **algebra**, both topics that you cover in your later high school years.

So why did it take so long for mathematicians to dig in to probability? In order to understand that, it is important to understand what it means for an event to be random. When you think of randomness, you probably think of events that you didn't see coming. Mathematicians define *random* as

ANCIENT ROMAN DICE GAMES WERE EVEN SHOWN IN THEIR MOSAIC ART.

"unable to be predicted for certain."

Mathematicians didn't always think of randomness like this, though. For a long time, until the 1500s, many mathematicians believed that the attitude of the person rolling the dice influenced which numbers would appear. They also believed strongly in luck and the idea of a higher power being in control of a particular event.

Such attitudes kept mathematicians from understanding the randomness of an event. However, in the 1500s, an Italian physician named Girolamo Cardano began to look at some of the math associated with rolling dice. Cardano loved to gamble and study math. He wrote a book based on some of his findings. *Liber de ludo aleae* (The book on games of chance), despite being written in the mid-1500s, was not published until 1663. Because the book was based on Cardano's interest in gambling, it was not always taken seriously as a math text.

As a result, French scholars Pierre de Fermat and Blaise Pascal are often considered the founders of modern probability, thanks to the work they did in the 1650s. They were not interested in shaking dice, though. They focused on how to divide the stakes, or winnings, of a game.

Imagine you and a friend are playing a game in which the winner will receive a $20 prize. You are flipping a coin. If the coin lands heads-up, you get a point; if it lands on tails, your friend gets the point. Unfortunately, you aren't able to finish the game before you have to go home. If you win two rounds and your friend wins one, how should you divide the prize?

That was the type of problem that interested Fermat and Pascal. Pascal looked at what might happen on the next flip. He considered the chances that you would win the round and the game (3–1). In this case, you would win the $20, and your friend would get nothing. He compared that situation against the chances of your friend's winning the round and the game finishing in a tie (2–2). If that were to occur, you and your friend would each get $10. Because the chance of a tie is greater, Pascal would have decided to give you $15 and your friend $5.

Pascal and Fermat were able to solve many other problems in probability. They began to realize that, although they could not predict *what* would happen, they could predict the *likelihood* of its happening. For instance, instead of saying with certainty that you would roll two sixes when you shook two dice, they were able to tell the chances of your getting two sixes.

(3-1)

~ PROBABILITY ~

(2-2)

Mathematicians after Fermat and Pascal relied on the idea of measuring the likelihood of an event. But probability was still rooted in **theory**. It didn't have the strong mathematical framework of algebra or **geometry**. That didn't come until 1933, when Russian mathematician Andrey Kolmogorov was able to develop a **set** of axioms, or basic ideas accepted as true. The simplest of these axioms defines events as members of a set, connecting the ideas of probability to an already established branch of math called set theory. Kolmogorov wrote *Foundations of the Theory of Probability* to outline these axioms. Publishing this book identified Kolmogorov as a world leader in probability.

At its roots, probability is a basis for solving problems. For example, mathematicians have recently helped doctors make decisions about vaccinating against smallpox by exploring the probability of an outbreak. They looked at the likelihood of the possible outcomes, and then they made decisions based on such information.

Statistics is a branch of math related to probability, but it involves collecting and analyzing **data** about situations that have occurred in order to make decisions about future events. Statisticians collect information about a given topic or experiment. They use that sample data and apply it to larger populations.

The first person to study statistics was an English shopkeeper named John Graunt. In 1603, 17 years before Graunt was born, churches in

England began issuing Bills of Mortality. These were weekly notices of the names of those of who had died in each parish, or group of churches. The process was started to help track the spread of illness, especially during outbreaks of plague. Graunt collected these documents and used the information about cause of death to do some of the first statistical analysis.

Graunt laid out the criteria for his questioning and then explained the results of his study. Graunt studied more than 229,250 deaths and especially examined murder. He showed that murder was not a common cause of death. By investigating how and when people died, he also observed how long they lived, so he became the first to use data to estimate life expectancy. Graunt predicted the chances that a person would survive to a particular age, combining probability with his work on statistics.

After Graunt, other mathematicians began collecting data on different events for use in making predictions. In the 1670s, English scientist Edmond Halley began researching the stars. Soon, he became interested in comets and used other astronomers' observations to calculate a comet's orbit. Then he was able to predict when the comet would appear again. Scientists are still able to predict when Halley's Comet, named after this mathematician, will reappear.

Mathematicians were interested in using statistics for the physical sciences, such as

CLOCKS THAT SIGNALED CHURCH SERVICES ALSO BECAME ASTRONOMICAL INSTRUMENTS.

physics and chemistry, because experiments in those sciences are easier to control. However, analyzing data from these experiments did not require complex calculations. The life sciences, such as biology, produced more complex data sets. In general, these sciences are more random.

An example of this can be found from 1919, when Ronald Fisher, a British statistician with an interest in farming, performed experiments designed to help farmers determine crop yield. Over the course of six years, Fisher was able to take data from his work with those farmers and write one of the best books on statistics. He looked at how to make conclusions using small amounts of data. While statisticians would prefer large amounts of information to analyze, this is not always possible. Fisher introduced ways for working with those smaller data sets, especially in cases where more data points could not be found.

Mathematicians continue to apply statistics in a variety of situations. For example, every 10 years, the United States takes a census, or a count of its people. This count gives the government information about how many people live in a particular area and what their backgrounds are like. Statisticians analyze this data and use it to make decisions, from the number of representatives a particular state should have in the federal government to the amount of money a community will receive for roads, hospitals, or housing.

Probability and statistics find many applications in daily life, from government services to kids on a playground shaking dice in a game of chance. Knowing how to predict potential outcomes before they occur as well as analyzing them afterward can be powerful tools—in the right hands.

Chances of Injury

What are the chances of being injured by a toilet or eaten by a shark? According to statisticians who continue to study the chances of numerous scenarios, you have a **1 in 10,000** chance of being injured by a toilet and a **1 in 3.7 million** chance of being eaten by a shark. While those odds seem pretty unlikely, you should know that the chances of winning the lottery are even less likely: **1 in 18.5 million!**

HOW CERTAIN IS IT?

IN ORDER TO DETERMINE PROBABILITY, YOU NEED TO FIRST understand the events that might occur. An event is a specific outcome, or result, of an experiment. For example, when you flip a coin, you are conducting an experiment in which the possible outcomes are heads or tails. Flipping heads would be an event that you might be observing. An event such as watching the weather could yield outcomes of anything from sun to rain to wind to clouds, and so on. Meteorologists, or scientists who study the weather, work closely with these events and the probability of particular weather systems and patterns.

Anyone who works with probability measures it with a **fraction** between zero and one. An event with a probability equal to zero will not happen. Can you think of any event that you know for certain won't happen? Even events such

as snow in July or your family's winning the lottery have slim chances. Their probability does not equal zero. In order to come up with an event that has a probability of zero, you may have to think outside the box. For example, if today is Tuesday, the probability of waking up tomorrow and finding out that it is Saturday is zero. That cannot happen.

On the other end of the probability spectrum are events with a probability of one. Those events will happen for certain. If today is Tuesday, then when you wake up tomorrow, it will be Wednesday. If you roll a die, you will end up with a number between one and six.

This measurement of probability as a number between zero and one helps to explain how you calculate it. Probability can be calculated for experiments in which each event is equally likely to occur. Equally likely events all have the same probability. Probability for such events is calculated using the following fraction.

Probability (Event) $= \dfrac{\text{(the number of desired outcomes)}}{\text{(the number of possible outcomes)}}$

"Probability" can be abbreviated as P, while "event" is abbreviated as E:

$$P\,(E)\ =\ \frac{\text{(desired outcomes)}}{\text{(total possible outcomes)}}$$

To use this fraction, you must first know what all the outcomes are. On page 17, there is an example for flipping a coin. When you flip a coin,

"HEADS" WON IN AN-
CIENT ROME BECAUSE
IT MEANT THE EMPEROR
AGREED WITH YOU.

How would the odds CHANGE IF YOU HAD two dice instead?

there are two possible outcomes—heads or tails. If you want to calculate the probability of flipping tails, there is one desired outcome.

$$P(\text{flipping tails}) = \frac{1}{2}$$

This fraction tells us that there is one way for a coin to land on tails out of two possible landings.

The easiest way to calculate probability is to first determine the value for the denominator, the bottom part of the fraction. You need to know how many total outcomes there are. Then, after you know those outcomes, determine how many outcomes are ones that you want, and use that number in the numerator, or the top part of the fraction. Calculate the probabilities of each event listed below.

Rolling a six on a die.
Picking a vowel out of all the possible letters.
Pulling a seven from a deck of cards. *

Calculating the probability of more challenging events becomes easier once you know all the possible outcomes. In that first example problem, you calculated the probability of rolling a six on one die. How would the odds change, if you had two dice instead?

To figure that out, you would first need to think of all the possible outcomes of rolling two dice. To make it a little easier, think of the dice as being different colors—for instance, green and purple. This will be helpful

Answer Key: Problem A

in distinguishing between two similar outcomes. For the purpose of calculating probability, rolling a six on the green die and a four on the purple die is a different outcome than rolling a four on the green die and a six on the purple die. The outcomes are listed below. (The first number of each pair represents the green die, and the purple die is second.)

1,1	1,2	1,3	1,4	1,5	1,6
2,1	2,2	2,3	2,4	2,5	2,6
3,1	3,2	3,3	3,4	3,5	3,6
4,1	4,2	4,3	4,4	4,5	4,6
5,1	5,2	5,3	5,4	5,5	5,6
6,1	6,2	6,3	6,4	6,5	6,6

There are 36 possible outcomes. How many of those outcomes have a six in them, whether it is on the green die or the purple die? The probability of rolling a six, when given two dice, is $11/36$. Now, using this table to guide you, calculate the probability of the following events.

Rolling a four on either die.
Rolling doubles (the same number).
Rolling a total of seven. *

The most common sum for two dice is seven. It occurs more often than any other sum. What would be the probability of not rolling a sum of seven? To calculate this, count up how many pairs do not equal seven. In calculating the probability of not rolling a total of seven, you are finding

*Answer Key: Problem B

Choose a Door

You are on a game show, looking at three closed doors. The host tells you to pick the one that has a car behind it. (The other two have goats behind them.) After you choose, he opens a different door, which has a goat behind it. He then offers you the chance to switch to the third door. This scenario is known as the "Monty Hall Problem." It is often studied in probability theory. According to the rules of probability, you should switch!

the probability of what is called the complement of the event. For a given event, the complement is all the outcomes that are undesirable and thus are not in the original event.

Together, the event and the complement represent all the possible outcomes of an experiment. This means that these two probabilities must add up to one.

$$P(Event) + P(Complement) = 1.$$

If you want to know the probability of just the complement of an event, you need only calculate the value of 1 - P(Event). For example, the probability of two dice adding up to be seven is $\frac{6}{36}$. To determine the probability of the complement, where the dice do not add up to seven, do the subtraction problem 1 - $\frac{6}{36}$. (Keep in mind that when subtracting with fractions, you first need to have common denominators!) That makes this problem $\frac{36}{36}$ - $\frac{6}{36}$, for a probability of $\frac{30}{36}$ or $\frac{5}{6}$.

Calculate the probability of the following complements to events. You have already calculated the probability of each event occurring.

Not rolling a six on a die.
Not picking a vowel out of all the possible letters.
Not pulling a seven from a deck of cards. *

In theory, an event's probability should always indicate how often it will occur. But in practice, the actual results can vary drastically. For example, in a bag of regular M&M's, there are six potential colors of M&M candies. Therefore, the probability of getting a blue M&M when you take one from a bag would be ⅙. However, sometimes the M&M's don't fit that theoretical probability.

Answer Key: Problem C

Imagine you grab a randomly chosen bag of M&M's from a supermarket shelf. When you dump out the M&M's to eat, you decide to use them as a study in probability. You notice that you have 11 red, 12 yellow, 15 blue, 9 green, 7 brown, and no orange. After checking to be sure that M&M's still include the color orange, you start to think about what happened.

You are studying the experimental probability of the event. Of those 54 M&M's, you expected to see 9 of each color (54 ÷ 6 = 9). That would be what should happen in theory, since there are six different colors. Yet your experiment revealed something different. Experimental probability is calculated with a different fraction.

$$P(Event) = \frac{\text{(number of times that event occurs)}}{\text{(number of trials in the experiment)}}$$

For your bag of M&M's, the experimental probability of getting a blue M&M is $^{15}\!/_{54}$, while the experimental probability of finding an orange M&M is $^{0}\!/_{54}$. Those are some strange results, but they are the results from your experiment. For experiments with such small sets of data, the experimental probability and theoretical probability are often very different. As you open more and more bags of M&M's, you will start to see that the experimental probability gets closer to the theoretical probability. Running more experiments like this is what statisticians do. They collect a lot of data, and then they look for what it tells them.

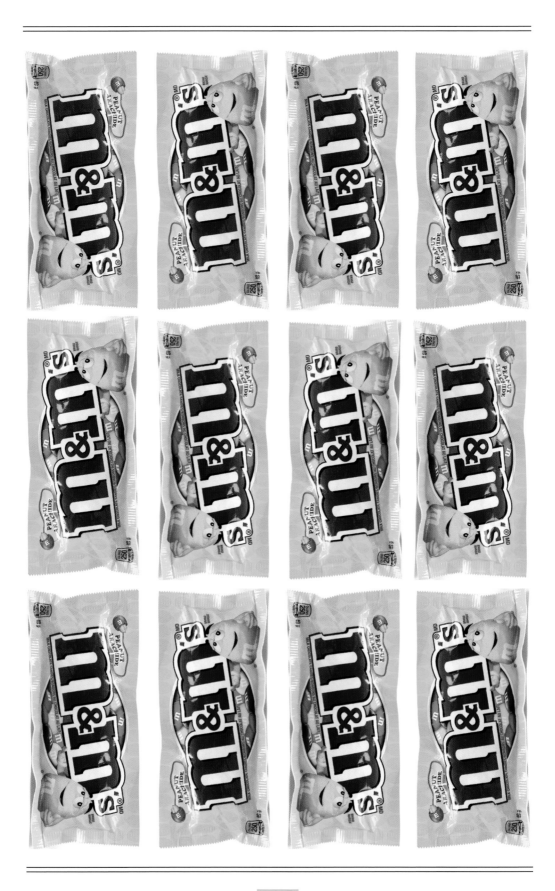

SAMPLES AND STUDIES

IN THAT M&M SCENARIO, YOU WERE PERFORMING AN EXPERIMENT USING a random bag of candies. Many times, mathematicians will conduct surveys to get the data they need. They have a specific population about which they are trying to gather data. However, instead of studying every member of a population, they take a sample.

In your M&M experiment, the population would be represented by every M&M to come out of the factory. It would take far too much time to count up that many chocolates! It's much easier to take a sample of those M&M's by looking at a bag. The sample was random; you just picked it out from the supermarket.

Random samples are just one type of sample that mathematicians can take when conducting a survey of a population. In a random sample, the participants or data points are chosen randomly. The idea is that every member of the population has the same chance

STATISTICS HELP YOU PREDICT WHICH COLOR APPEARS MOST OFTEN IN A BAG OF M&M'S.

of being picked. An example of a random selection would be opening a phone book to any page and picking a name off that page to interview.

Mathematicians can also use a systematic sample. This is when the first member of a study or survey is chosen at random and then all following members are chosen according to a system. The system is predetermined by the researchers, and it is usually calculated by dividing the number of people in the total population by the number of people needed for the study. For example, if a mathematician wanted to study weather patterns in a given year by using a sample size of 120 days, she would choose to examine every third day. The sample would start with a random day, and then continue every third day after that.

A self-selecting sample is one in which participants choose to respond to the question at hand. Voting in an election is a type of self-selecting sample. People have the opportunity to cast a **ballot** on a specific topic. However, if they don't want to vote, they don't have to do so.

A final type of sample for data collection is the convenience sample. In

this sample, the person conducting the survey chooses participants based on what is easiest for him- or herself. Your M&M experiment could be described as a convenience sample. The bag of chocolates that you chose probably came from the supermarket closest to you. You picked one that was convenient.

When mathematicians use samples to represent larger data populations, they hope that the sample will accurately represent the population as a whole. Unfortunately, this does not always occur. Sometimes the sample is skewed, favoring one side or the other. For example, if you went to a local football game and asked fans whether the team needed a new stadium to play in, you might receive an overwhelmingly positive response. But if you asked the same question of people at the supermarket, they might not feel as strongly. In this case, the location of the audience could have skewed the results of the survey.

Moreover, the way a particular question is framed, or asked, can swing the results one way or another. Sometimes surveys ask questions that are biased. Biased questions tend to lead a responder to pick a particular type of answer. Returning to the stadium example, read through the following questions to see if you can spot the biased view:

"Do you think the football team needs a new stadium?"

"Do you think your hard-earned money should pay for a new stadium for the football team?"

SWING *THE* RESULTS ONE WAY OR ANOTHER

Putting the phrase "your hard-earned money" in the question makes the second one biased. The surveyor is trying to make responders feel as though they shouldn't have to use their own money to fund the stadium. The question becomes personal. As you read through the following questions, try to identify the phrase that makes the question appear biased. How would you rephrase the question to remove the bias?

- **Since cigarettes are dangerous to all people, do you believe they should be outlawed?**
- **Should the beautiful, historic theater be demolished to put up an ugly strip mall?**
- **Considering how slow a baseball game is, would you rather watch baseball or football on TV? ***

Biased questions are worded in such a way as to prevent their results from being accurate. However, when mathematicians are able to collect unbiased data from an accurate sample, that data can be very useful. Before even analyzing it with calculations, mathematicians can look at a visual representation of data—such as a graph—to get some basic information.

Graphs can show information about such things as frequency, trends over time, or patterns in the results. Bar graphs, double bar graphs, and line graphs are just three of the types that represent data in a visual way. Other graphs are helpful in exploring data that is better analyzed by looking at the numbers.

Bar graphs use vertical or horizontal bars to show the quantities of various sets. They can be used to compare frequency among different groups. If you plotted the results of your M&M experiment on a bar graph, you would be able to see which color occurred most often. If you were to go out and buy another bag of M&M's, you could use a double bar graph to compare the quantities of both bags and compare the color frequencies between the two bags. Look at the two representations opposite.

*Answer Key: Problem D

M & M Experiment Results: ONE BAG

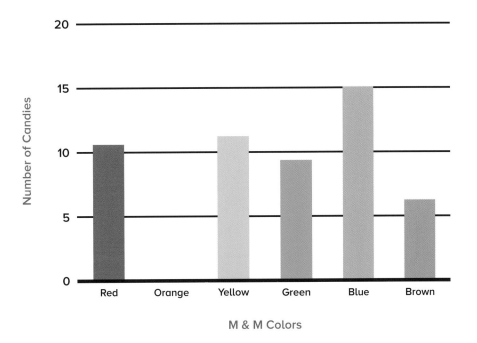

M & M Experiment Results: TWO BAGS

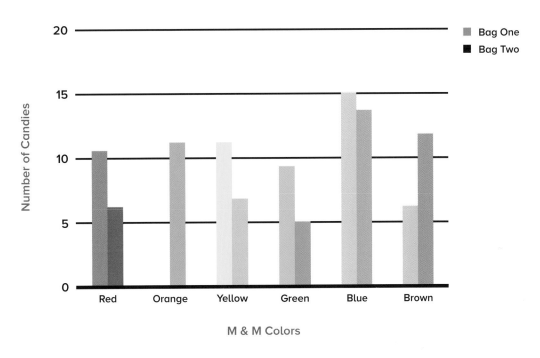

Another type of graph is used to examine how data changes over time. A line graph connects points that represent quantities as measured at particular times. Picture a line graph as being like a bar graph. Instead of drawing in the bars, you could just connect the tops of each bar with a line. This type of graph would be helpful in charting U.S. census results since 1900. By connecting the data points, you could easily see how the population has changed from one census year to the next. Moreover, you could also predict future populations based on trends or patterns shown.

U.S. POPULATION

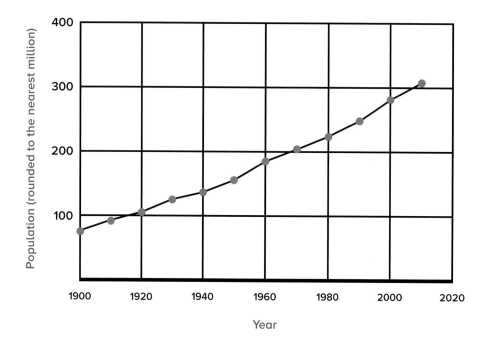

CONNECT *the* DATA POINTS

Graphs such as line plots or stem-and-leaf plots can be easy ways to reference the raw numbers of a particular data set. To draw a line plot, mathematicians start with a number line. The number line begins with the lowest value in the data set and ends with the highest value. All values in between are then filled in on the number line. Stem-and-leaf plots break up each data point and show the frequency of different values. For example,

People look at GRAPHS TO MAKE *inferences*

the tens digit of a number is used as a stem. Any number that has that digit in its tens place will be a leaf on that stem. Leaves are represented using the ones digit. The same data set is illustrated below using both plotting methods. The numbers represent scores on a test that was worth 50 points.

{39, 40, 36, 40, 42, 34, 42, 40, 34, 36, 40, 38, 40, 46, 36, 40, 46, 46, 26, 32, 48, 46, 34, 50, 20}

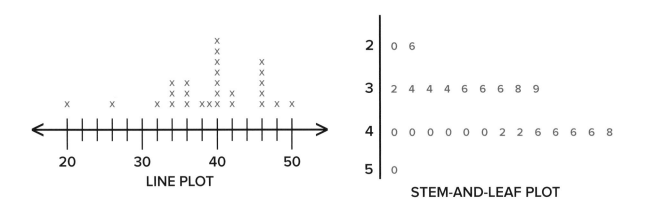

LINE PLOT

STEM-AND-LEAF PLOT

What did you notice in each graph? It may have been easier to see the most common score on the line plot, but in the stem-and-leaf plot, you probably noticed which score range was most common.

All these graphs can be used to represent data before any calculations happen. People look at graphs to make inferences, or predict what will happen in the future. Once all the unbiased data has been collected and represented, that's where statistics comes in.

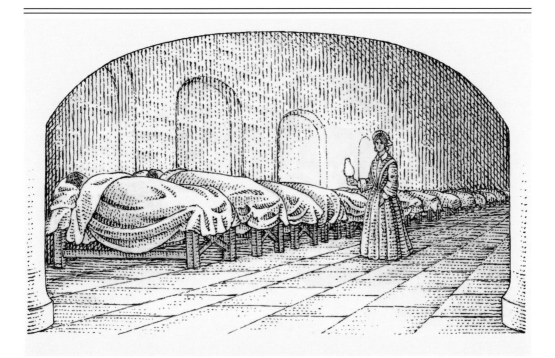

FIGURE IT OUT!

Diagrams for Life

In the **1850s**, British nurse Florence Nightingale used her love of mathematics and knowledge of statistics to improve conditions for wounded soldiers. She collected data on mortality rates, studying how improving cleanliness in hospitals would save more lives. She then represented the findings graphically in **polar area diagrams**. Her statistical work helped convince lawmakers to make changes that decreased the mortality rate in field hospitals by more than **50 percent**.

MEASURING
TENDENCIES

1 2 3 4 5 6 7 8 9 10 11 12 13 14 15 16 17 18 19 20 21 22 23 24 25

WHEN PEOPLE USE MATHEMATICS AND CALCULATIONS TO ANALYZE data, they become statisticians. Statistics is about taking data and information and looking for patterns within it. It is not enough to simply gather the data, and then let it sit. Statisticians manipulate data to make it tell them things. They can use it to predict what will happen next or to understand what happened in a given situation.

> MEASUREMENTS TAKEN WITH A RULER ARE MUCH DIFFERENT FROM THOSE USING STATS.

When your class takes a test during the year, your teacher gets the results. She may compare the high scores with the low scores to understand why different students earned different scores. If many students got the same questions wrong, she may consider how to improve her teaching of that topic. The average score of the entire class might give her a sense of how well the class as a whole knows the material. When your teacher is doing these things, she is acting and thinking like a statistician.

Some of the most common information pulled from a data set are the measures of central tendency known as mean, median, mode, and range. These types of measures tell you about the middle value of your data set and act as a snapshot of the data points.

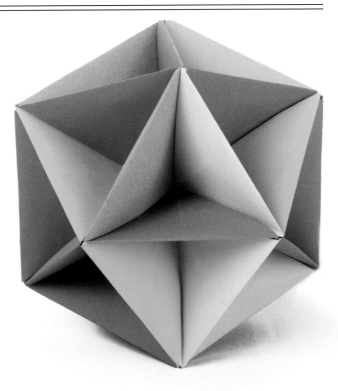

The mean is the average of the data set. In order to calculate the mean, you add up each data point, and then divide by how many points there are. The median is the middle of the points. To find the median, you should list all the numbers in order from smallest to largest. If you cross out one number at a time from each edge, you will work your way in toward the middle. The number that is left when all others have been eliminated is the median. (If you end up with two numbers, you can add them together and divide by

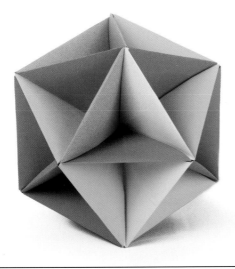

two.) The third measure of central tendency is the mode. The mode is the value that occurs most often. Organizing the data for finding the median will also help you find the mode, because all the numbers are grouped already. The range shows the spread of data. It tells you if the data is huddled around the same points or if the values are spread out.

You can calculate the mean, median, and mode for any data set, no matter how large it is. Imagine that your math class had a quiz. Below is the set of scores from that quiz. The quiz had a possible high score of 20 points. Follow along with the steps provided to find the mean, median, mode, and range of the data.

{15, 18, 10, 17, 15, 20, 15, 9, 18, 19, 16, 16, 16, 17, 14, 15, 20, 6, 18, 17, 14, 15, 18, 19, 13, 17, 18, 19}

To find the mean, begin by adding up all the scores:

15 + 18 + 10 + 17 + 15 + 20 + 15 + 9 + 18 + 19 + 16 + 16 + 16 + 17 + 14 + 15 + 20 + 6 + 18 + 17 + 14 + 5 + 18 + 19 + 13 + 17 + 18 + 19 = 444

Divide the total of the scores (444) by 28, the number of scores listed. Your answer should be rounded to the nearest hundredth.

$$444 \div 28 = 15.86$$

The mean is 15.86, so the class average on this quiz was 15.86, equal to 79.30 percent. To find the median, begin by listing the numbers in order from smallest to largest:

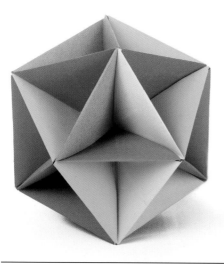

6, 9, 10, 13, 14, 14, 15, 15, 15, 15, 15, 16, 16, 16, 17, 17, 17, 17, 18, 18, 18, 18, 18, 19, 19, 19, 20, 20

Next, cross out pairs of numbers, one from each end of the list. This will leave

Statistics show up in nearly every area of life. As coaches help their teams win, they analyze players to determine if they are performing the way they should. Healthcare officials use statistics to predict what types of illnesses might show up in a given place. Computer programmers use statistics to calculate how often an idea shows up in an Internet search. No matter what you are interested in, statistics can be used to study it!

you with two numbers, 16 and 17. Add those two numbers together, and divide their sum by two.

$$16 + 17 = 33$$
$$33 \div 2 = 16.5$$

The median of this data set is 16.5.

Now that the data is listed in order, you can see all the numbers and their duplicates. To find the mode, locate the numbers that occur most often. At first glance, it looks as though 15, 17, and 18 occur the greatest number of times. If you count them up, 15 appears 5 times, 17 appears 4 times, and 18 appears 5 times. As a result, 15 and 18 are the modes. (It's okay to have more than one mode in a data set. It's also okay for a data set to have no mode.)

Again using the order in which you placed the scores to find the median, you'll be able to figure out the range. Subtract the smallest value (6) from the largest value (20). The answer (14) will be the range.

$$20 - 6 = 14$$

Calculate the mean, median, mode, and range of the following data sets.

Your teacher surveys your class, asking how many kids are in your family. Here are the results of her survey: {3, 3, 2, 2, 8, 4, 6, 8, 5, 4, 2, 1, 3, 3, 2, 3, 2, 3, 2, 2, 3, 2}

The number of points your basketball team scored in its last 12 games is given in this set: {28, 30, 38, 24, 29, 40, 37, 33, 26, 18, 31, 19} *

In some data sets, there is a data point that is very different from the others. This is most easily seen when a data set has a wide range. When this happens, your data is said to have an outlier, a value that is far less or far greater than the other points.

In looking at the quiz score example from earlier, there is a point that could be considered an outlier. Can you recognize it? Here's a hint: often an outlier may be the minimum or maximum value of a set. In the case of the quiz scores, the maximum (20) is not an outlier, because there are plenty of other data points that are close to it. The minimum value (6) is the outlier. It is the farthest away from the rest of the data points.

CALCULATE THE
MEAN, MODE, AND RANGE OF THE DATA SETS

*Answer Key: Problem E

Conversations about DATA IS WHAT STATISTICS *is all about!*

Can you identify the outlier in the following data sets?

The temperature (in degrees Fahrenheit) of a city was measured for 10 consecutive days during winter: {7, 1, 1, 0, 28, 37, -2, -11, 5, 0}

The number of homework problems that your teacher has assigned you in the last three weeks: {15, 18, 6, 30, 27, 30, 21, 31, 23, 28} *

It is important to be able to recognize outliers because they can skew the measures of central tendency. Skewed measures can lead to incorrect predictions or assumptions. Removing an outlier can provide more accurate measures. If you throw out the outlier (6) from the quiz scores, the measures of central tendency change. The new mean becomes 16.22, bringing the average test score up a whole letter grade. The new median is 17, and the range is now 11. The mode does not change, though.

You may have noticed that the mean and range change the most with the removal of outliers. Therefore, they may not be the best options for discussing data. The mean can be pulled in the direction of the outlier, as that number can impact the sum of the numbers in the set. However, the median is not impacted in that way, so it can be used as a truer representative of the data.

Back in his day, Ronald Fisher explained how to work with both large

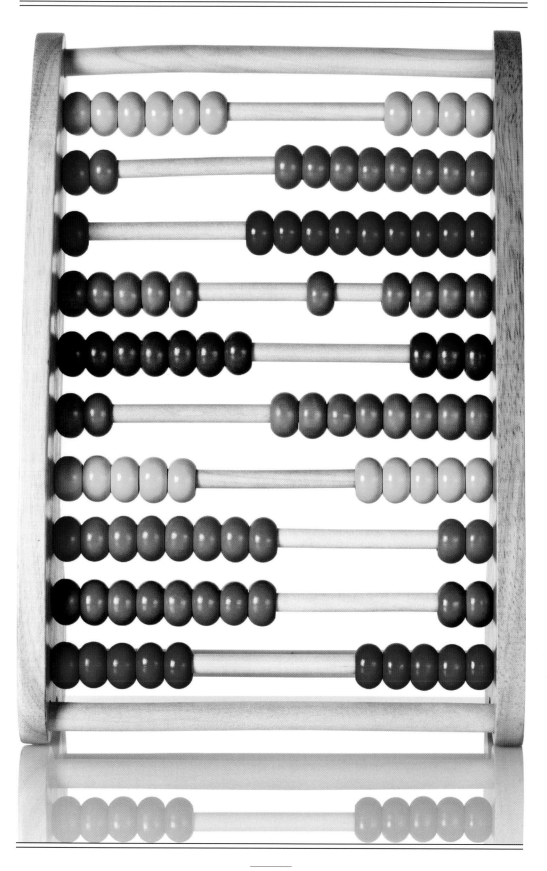

and small data sets. While large data sets paint a clearer picture of the information, it can be tough to sort through all those numbers. By calculating the measures of central tendency, data can be discussed in more bite-sized portions. And after all, conversations about data is what statistics is all about!

MATH TOOLKIT

1. Dice are frequently used in board games because they are fair, meaning that each number has the same chance of being rolled. This characteristic is what makes dice useful for studying probability, too. Before dice, ancient Egyptians shook astragali, which were the heel bones of different animals. Because of the differences in age, size, or species of the animals, the astragali produced different results. Until fair dice were invented, data could not be collected reliably—and probability couldn't be developed.

2. To count the possible outcomes for their event, statisticians rely on the Fundamental Counting Principle. This tool multiplies the number of choices for the first item by the number of choices for the second item, and so on. Imagine that you are creating an ice cream sundae and can choose from eight ice cream flavors, three sauces, six candy toppings, and four fruits. If you have to choose one of each type, the Fundamental Counting Principle shows that there are 576 combinations possible!

3. Ronald Fisher believed that a successful experiment depended on the way questions were asked. In an article called "Mathematics of a Lady Tasting Tea," Fisher laid out the complications of designing effective experiments. He introduced the concept of changing only the part of the experiment being studied, keeping everything else the same as it was in a control experiment. Any changes in the data must then be the effects of that change.

4. Statisticians find outliers first by determining the median of the lower (Q_1) and upper (Q_3) halves of their data set. Those numbers are used to calculate the interquartile range ($IQR = Q_3 - Q_1$). Outliers are numbers whose values are less than $Q_1 - 1.5(IQR)$ or greater than $Q_3 + 1.5(IQR)$. In the following example of test scores, the IQR is 3: 6, 9, 10, 13, 14, 14, 15, 15, 15, 15, 15, 16, 16, 16, 17, 17, 17, 17, 18, 18, 18, 18, 18, 19, 19, 19, 20, 20. $Q_1 = 15$ and $Q_3 = 18$. Any outliers are less than $15 - 1.5(3) = 15 - 4.5 = 10.5$ or greater than $18 + 1.5(3) = 18 + 4.5 = 22.5$. This data set has three outliers: 6, 9, and 10.

GLOSSARY

algebra: a branch of mathematics that uses letters and numbers to solve for un-known values in different equations

ballot: a form used for casting votes through writing

calculations: operations performed on numbers

data: facts and information collected for the purpose of being studied

fraction: a number that relates pieces of a whole quantity by division

geometry: a branch of mathematics that works with the properties of shapes

polar area diagrams: forms of pie charts in which all sections have the same angle

sets: collections of numbers that belong together because of certain characteristics

theory: an idea that is presented as probably true but has not yet been proven

trigonometry: a branch of mathematics that studies the side lengths and angle measures of triangles

SELECTED BIBLIOGRAPHY

Berlinghoff, William P., and Fernando Q. Gouvêa. *Math through the Ages: A Gentle History for Teachers and Others.* Washington, D.C.: MAA Service Center, 2004.

Mackenzie, Dana. *What's Happening in the Mathematical Sciences.* 9 vols. Providence, R.I.: American Mathematical Society, 2013.

O'Connor, John J., and Edmund F. Robertson. "Nightingale Biography." MacTutor History of Mathematics Archive. http://www.history.mcs.st-and.ac.uk/Biographies /Nightingale.html.

Raedle, Joe. "Feeling Lucky? How Lotto Odds Compare to Shark Attacks and Lightning Strikes." *National Geographic Daily News,* December 19, 2013. http://news .nationalgeographic.com/news/2013/12/131219-lottery-odds-winning-mega-million-lotto/.

Rooney, Anne. *The Story of Mathematics.* London: Arcturus, 2008.

Struik, Dirk J. *A Concise History of Mathematics.* New York: Dover, 1987.

Tabak, John. *Probability & Statistics: The Science of Uncertainty.* New York: Checkmark Books, 2005.

WEBSITES

Data Domain
http://kids.nceas.ucsb.edu/DataandScience/datadomain.html
Use the scientific method and ecological information to study data collection in experiments.

Stay or Switch: The Monty Hall Problem
http://stayorswitch.com/explanation.php
Experience the Monty Hall Problem firsthand, and choose a solution.

Note: Every effort has been made to ensure that the websites listed above are suitable for children, that they have educational value, and that they contain no inappropriate material. However, because of the nature of the Internet, it is impossible to guarantee that these sites will remain active indefinitely or that their contents will not be altered.

INDEX

ANSWER KEY

Problem A

Probability of rolling a six on a die:

      Desired outcomes: one {6}

      Total outcomes: six

      P(rolling a six) = 1/6

Probability of picking a vowel out of all the possible letters:

      Desired outcomes: five {a, e, i, o, and u}

      Total outcomes: 26

      P(picking a vowel) = 5/26

Probability of pulling a seven from a deck of cards:

      Desired outcomes: four {hearts, diamonds, spades, clubs}

      Total outcomes: 52

      P(pulling a seven) = 4/52 = 1/13

Problem B

Probability of rolling a four on either die:

      Desired outcomes: 11 {(1,4), (2,4), (3,4), (5,4), (6,4), (4,1), (4,2), (4,3),

          (4,5), (4,6), (4,4)}

      Total outcomes: 36

      P(rolling a four on either die) = 11/36

Probability of rolling doubles (the same number):

      Desired outcomes: six {(1,1), (2,2), (3,3), (4,4), (5,5), (6,6)}

      Total outcomes: 36

      P(rolling doubles) = 6/36 = 1/6

Probability of rolling a total of seven:

      Desired outcomes: six {(1,6), (2,5), (3,4), (4,3), (5,2), (6,1)}

      Total outcomes: 36

      P(rolling a total of seven) = 6/36 = 1/6

Problem C

Probability of not rolling a six on a die:

P(Complement) = 1 - *P(Event)*

P(not rolling a six) = 1 - $\frac{1}{6}$

P(not rolling a six) = $\frac{6}{6}$ - $\frac{1}{6}$

P(not rolling a six) = $\frac{5}{6}$

Probability of not picking a vowel out of all the possible letters:

P(Complement) = 1 - *P(Event)*

P(not picking a vowel) = 1 - $\frac{5}{26}$

P(not picking a vowel) = $\frac{26}{26}$ - $\frac{5}{26}$

P(not picking a vowel) = $\frac{21}{26}$

Probability of not pulling a seven from a deck of cards:

P(Complement) = 1 - *P(Event)*

P(not pulling a seven) = 1 - $\frac{1}{13}$

P(not pulling a seven) = $\frac{13}{13}$ - $\frac{1}{13}$

P(not pulling a seven) = $\frac{12}{13}$

Problem D

Since cigarettes are dangerous to all people, do you believe that they should be outlawed?

A possible revision might be, "Should cigarettes be made illegal?" Should the beautiful, historic theater be demolished to put up an ugly strip mall?

A possible revision might be, "What are your thoughts about building a strip mall where the theater was?"

Considering how slow a baseball game is, would you rather watch baseball or football on TV?

A possible revision might be, "Would you rather watch baseball or football on TV?"

Problem E

Your teacher surveys your class, asking how many kids are in your family. Here are the results of her survey:

{3, 3, 2, 2, 8, 4, 6, 8, 5, 4, 2, 1, 3, 3, 2, 3, 2, 3, 2, 2, 3, 2}

Mean: 3 + 3 + 2 + 2 + 8 + 4 + 6 + 8 + 5 + 4 + 2 + 1 + 3 + 3 + 2 + 3 +

     2 + 3 + 2 + 2 + 3 + 2 = 73

     73 ÷ 22 = 3.32

     The mean is 3.32.

Median: 1, 2, 2, 2, 2, 2, 2, 2, 2, 3, 3, 3, 3, 3, 3, 3, 4, 4, 5, 6, 8, 8

     The median is 3.

Mode: The mode is 2.

Range: 8 - 1 = 7

     The range is 7.

The number of points your basketball team scored in its last 12 games is given in this set:

{28, 30, 38, 24, 29, 40, 37, 33, 26, 18, 31, 19}

     Mean: 28 + 30 + 38 + 24 + 29 + 40 + 37 + 33 + 26 + 18 + 31 + 19 = 353

     353 ÷ 12 = 29.42

     The mean is 29.42.

     Median: 18, 19, 24, 26, 28, 29, 30, 31, 33, 37, 38, 40

     29 + 30 = 59. 59 ÷ 2 = 29.5

     The median is 29.5.

     Mode: There is no mode.

     Range: 40 - 18 = 22

     The range is 22.

Problem F

The temperature (in degrees Fahrenheit) of a city was measured for 10 consecutive days during winter:

{7, 1, 1, 0, 28, 37, -2, -11, 5, 0}

     Two outliers are 28 and 37.

The number of homework problems that your teacher has assigned you in the last three weeks:

{15, 18, 6, 30, 27, 30, 21, 31, 23, 28}

     The outlier is 6.